NATURE'S CHILDREN

SHARKS

by *Katie Marsico*

Content Consultant
Dr. Stephen S. Ditchkoff
Professor of Wildlife Sciences
Auburn University
Auburn, Alabama

Photographs © 2012: age fotostock: 23 (Reinhard Dirscherl),
39 (Tom Campbell); Alamy Images: 16, 32 (Brandon Cole Marine
Photography), 5 bottom, 35 (imagebroker), 28 (Mark Conlin); Bob
Italiano: 44 foreground, 45 foreground; Dreamstime: 2 background,
3 background, 44 background, 45 background (Joao Estevao
Andrade De Freitas), cover (Photomyeye); Getty Images: 36 (Andy
Murch/Visuals Unlimited, Inc.), 31 (Ethan Miller); iStockphoto/
Krzysztof Odziomek: 24; Minden Pictures/Chris Newbert: 19;
Shutterstock, Inc.: 27 (A Cotton Photo), 20 (FAUP), 1, 2 foreground,
3 foreground, 4, 5 background, 12 (Ian Scott), 8 (JonMilnes), 15
(stockpix4u), 40 (tororo reaction), 7 (tubuceo); Superstock/age
fotostock: 5 top, 11.

Library of Congress Cataloging-in-Publication Data
Marsico, Katie, 1980–
    Sharks/by Katie Marsico.
        p. cm.–(Nature's children)
    Includes bibliographical references and index.
    ISBN-13: 978-0-531-20907-3 (lib. bdg.)
        ISBN-10: 0-531-20907-5 (lib. bdg.)
    ISBN-13: 978-0-531-21082-6 (pbk.)
        ISBN-10: 0-531-21082-0 (pbk.)
    1. Sharks—Juvenile literature. I. Title. II. Series.
    QL638.9.M287 2012
    597.3—dc23   2011031083

All rights reserved. Published in 2012 by Children's Press, an imprint
of Scholastic Inc.
Printed in China 62
SCHOLASTIC, CHILDREN'S PRESS, and associated logos are
trademarks and/or registered trademarks of Scholastic Inc.

1 2 3 4 5 6 7 8 9 10 R 21 20 19 18 17 16 15 14 13 12

Sharks

Class	Chondrichthyes
Orders	Eight orders
Families	Around 30 families
Genera	More than 100 genera
Species	About 400 species, including great white sharks, whale sharks, and hammerheads
World distribution	All of the world's oceans
Habitat	Shallow, deep, and open waters; most sharks live in saltwater environments; some have adapted to freshwater
Distinctive physical characteristics	Streamlined shape and strong tail; 5 to 15 rows of teeth; skeleton made mostly of cartilage; both upper and lower jaws are movable
Habits	Typically not territorial; migratory and able to adapt to new environments; not likely to care for young after either laying eggs or giving live birth
Diet	Most eat fish, squid, crustaceans, and sometimes birds and mammals; filter feeders' diets are mainly made up of plankton

Contents

CHAPTER 1

Underwater Predators

Swimmers fear them. Scientists are fascinated by them. Sharks have swum in Earth's oceans for hundreds of millions of years. Yet people are still hunting for clues that will help them learn more about these amazing underwater predators.

Not all sharks are alike. There are about 400 different species. The pale catshark is only 8.27 inches (22 centimeters) long. This is only a little longer than a sharpened pencil! The whale shark, however, measures about 40 feet (12 meters) in length. This is about the size of a school bus.

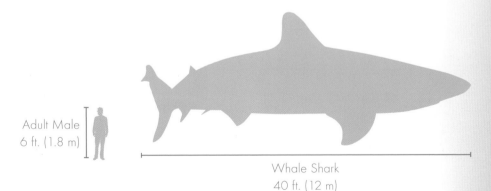

Adult Male
6 ft. (1.8 m)

Whale Shark
40 ft. (12 m)

Scientists dive deep underwater to see how sharks live in the wild.

Intelligence and Instinct

Most scientists think that sharks are fairly intelligent. Some sharks are even smart enough to work together as a team to locate prey. This behavior is a clue that they have problem-solving skills. People are beginning to understand that sharks are not just mindless monsters. They are skilled hunters whose brains have helped them survive for millions of years.

Sharks also have strong instincts. For example, they will migrate to new locations if their food supply begins running low in certain areas. Some even travel hundreds of miles to find their next meal!

 **FUN FACT!** Great white sharks can sense blood in the water from 3 miles (5 kilometers) away.

Sharks are far more than fierce killers.

CHAPTER 2

Built to Be Survivors

Experts believe that sharks existed even before dinosaurs walked the earth! How have sharks managed to survive this long when other animals, such as dinosaurs, have not?

Sharks' bodies are just as incredible as their intelligence and instincts. Most sharks are streamlined. Their shape allows them to move smoothly and easily through the water. This helps increase their speed as they swim and chase prey.

Most fish have skeletons made of bones and a tough elastic tissue called cartilage. But sharks only have bones in their jaws. The rest of their skeleton is made of cartilage. Having more bones would make sharks heavier. This would slow them down as they swam. Having a skeleton made of cartilage also allows sharks to be more flexible as they glide through the water.

Their cartilage allows sharks more freedom of movement.

Fins and Tails

People who spot these fish are usually both terrified and curious when they see dorsal fins cutting through the waves. The dorsal fin is on top of the shark's body. It gives the shark balance and stability. But this fin is just one of several different fins on a shark. A pair of pectoral fins is located near the bottom front of the shark's body. These fins help the shark lift its body and steer through the water.

Sharks also have strong tails to help them move easily through water. Their tails are different shapes and sizes, depending on the type of shark. Some sharks' tails help them to move fast to catch speedy prey. Other sharks use their tails to twist and turn to find food.

The blacktip reef shark has dark coloring on the tips of its fins.

13

Sharks' Skin

Even a shark's skin is designed to help it move through the water. Shark skin is made up of scales called dermal denticles. These particles are almost like tiny teeth. Dermal denticles point toward the shark's tail. This reduces the friction between a shark's skin and the water. Another way dermal denticles reduce friction is they keep algae and barnacles from sticking to the shark's skin. Less friction means that sharks can swim more easily.

Shark skin feels as rough as sandpaper if someone rubs it in the opposite direction from the way the dermal denticles are pointing.

Zebra sharks have spotted skin that helps them blend in with the ocean floor.

Biting

A swiftly moving shark is a terrifying sight for any animals that these fierce fish eat. One look inside a shark's mouth can show you why! Sharks usually have 5 to 15 rows of teeth in each jaw. The teeth easily fall out. Yet they are also easily replaced. Scientists have learned that a shark can replace a lost tooth in just 24 hours.

Shark teeth come in several different shapes and sizes. Some are extremely sharp and serrated like a steak knife. Many sharks use their teeth to bite and tear apart prey. Sharks also have unique jaws. Most animals can only move their lower jaw to grab prey. Sharks can move both their upper and lower jaws. This is because their jaws aren't attached to a bony skeleton. A shark can use its entire tooth-lined mouth to grab and devour food.

Many sharks have razor-sharp teeth.

Exceptional Senses

Sharks also rely on other parts of their bodies to survive in Earth's oceans. Scientists know that these fish have sharp eyesight. Their eyes are sensitive to light and color. This helps them spot prey as they swim at different depths in the water.

Sharks have good hearing, too. Their ears are inside of their heads. They use them to hear distant sounds. Sharks rely on their excellent hearing to pick up vibrations in the water that occur when fish splash and swim.

They also use a special sense organ called a lateral line to pick up vibrations. A shark's lateral line is made up of nerve cells that stretch along its sides and into its head. The lateral line detects vibrations and changes in water pressure. This lets the shark know when there are other fish swimming nearby.

Sharks roll their eyes back into their heads when feeding to prevent damage from resistant prey.

Breathing and Hiding

Sharks depend on their nostrils to pick up smells from hundreds of yards away. But they do not use these nostrils to breathe. Instead, sharks rely on openings behind their head called gills. Water passes into the mouth and through the gills. A shark's blood vessels take oxygen out of the water. This allows the shark to breathe. Yet it is also what makes most sharks stay on the move. Many species must swim without stopping for water to keep passing through their gills.

Countershading is another unique feature that helps many sharks hunt prey and avoid predators. Countershading is when fish have darker coloring on their top side than their underside. The different colors become a kind of camouflage for sharks. This is because different parts of the ocean have different levels of light. Countershading makes sharks hard to spot from both above and below. It is one of the many reasons that sharks have been able to survive in Earth's oceans for millions of years!

Some sharks are almost completely white on their undersides.

CHAPTER 3

A Shark's Life

Sharks live in all of the world's oceans. They can be spotted everywhere from tropical reefs in the Caribbean Sea to the icy waters of the North Pole. Most species are found in salt water. A few, such as the bull shark, have learned to **adapt** to freshwater lakes and rivers.

Different species have adapted to different underwater **environments**. The nurse shark prefers warm, shallow waters. Goblin sharks swim hundreds of feet beneath the waves. They can survive in parts of the ocean that are so deep even the rays of the sun do not light or warm the water.

Bull sharks have learned to adapt to multiple environments.

Different Diets

What sharks eat depends on a few things. Different species have different diets. A shark's food source is also affected by where it is hunting.

Many sharks have a diet that is made up of fish, squid, and crustaceans. Yet every species prefers certain foods. For example, tiger sharks often hunt sea turtles. Great white sharks are known to eat everything from seals to dolphins to penguins. Their serrated teeth rip into the flesh of whatever fish, mammal, or bird they are attacking.

Most sharks do not hunt humans. They often confuse surfers and swimmers with other prey. Unfortunately, shark attacks on humans still do occur from time to time. But they do not happen very often.

Some species, such as the whale shark, are filter feeders. These sharks simply open their mouths and use special gill plates to filter through the water that flows inside. Filter feeders use their gills to catch tiny sea creatures called plankton. Sharks that feed this way often filter hundreds of thousands of gallons of water every hour!

The whale shark is the largest living fish, but it eats only tiny sea animals.

Hunting in Packs

Scientists do not believe that sharks are territorial. This is because most species often travel in search of food. They do not usually have a single stretch of water that they view as being only their hunting ground. Many species even hunt or migrate together.

Sharks do not fight over space. But they do often fight over prey. Sharks can become extremely aggressive during a feeding frenzy. They fight and sometimes kill each other when more than one shark is after the same piece of food.

FUN FACT! People are more likely to be killed by insects or dogs than they are by sharks.

Sharks sometimes even eat each other during feeding frenzies.

Shark Babies

Sharks can be born in different ways. Some sharks lay eggs in protective cases. These cases are often called mermaid's purses. The babies eventually hatch and swim into the ocean. Other sharks give birth to live young called pups.

Different species of sharks carry their eggs or babies inside them for varying periods of time. Some mother sharks carry the eggs or babies for four or five months. Others keep their eggs or babies inside them for up to two years.

Some sharks produce only one pup at a time. Others have more than 100. Mother sharks do not usually care for the pups. It is up to young sharks to survive on their own in the world's oceans!

FUN FACT! A single shark can shed as many as 50,000 teeth throughout its lifetime.

Egg cases are made of tough protective material.

CHAPTER 4

Sharks in the Past and Present

Scientists believe that sharks have lived on Earth for 350 million to 450 million years. The earliest fossils of shark teeth date back about 400 million years. Scientists who have studied shark fossils believe that many species once roamed prehistoric seas.

It is important to keep in mind that not all of these animals looked like modern sharks. Many early species were much smaller than today's sharks. Their teeth were smoother. Early sharks also had more rounded noses and smaller brains. Sharks that are more similar to modern species began to appear about 100 million years ago.

One of the most famous prehistoric sharks was called megalodon. This giant fish appeared about 16 million years ago and disappeared about 14 million years later. Megalodon measured 50 feet (15 m) long and weighed 52 tons (47,000 kilograms). Scientists believe megalodon may have been the earliest ancestor of the great white shark.

Megalodon is bigger than any other known shark species.

The Great White Shark

The great white is probably one of the most famous modern species of shark. About one-third to one-half of all shark attacks on humans come from great whites. These sharks can grow to more than 20 feet (6.1 m) in length. They can weigh more than 5,000 pounds (2,268 kg). They can swim as fast as 15 miles (24 km) per hour.

Their size, speed, and terrifying jaws make them ferocious hunters. Great whites prefer to feed on sea lions, seals, smaller whales, and sea turtles. They are found worldwide but mainly live in the Atlantic, Indian, and Pacific Oceans.

Great whites are the largest predatory fish in the world. But they are not the largest sharks. Whale sharks are even larger!

Great white sharks can launch themselves out of the water to capture prey.

Whale Sharks and Hammerheads

Whale sharks measure about 40 feet (12 m) long and weigh 15 tons (13,608 kg) on average. These sharks also live in the Atlantic, Indian, and Pacific Oceans.

Whale sharks are huge. But they are far from vicious. They eat mostly plankton. Some are even gentle enough to allow divers to swim alongside them.

Swimmers would not want to try this with hammerhead sharks. These sharks are much smaller than whale sharks but are aggressive predators. What makes hammerheads most famous are their oddly shaped heads. They have flat heads that stretch outward on either side like a hammer. Most hammerheads live in the Atlantic, Indian, and Pacific Oceans.

Hammerheads sometimes use their heads to pin prey to the ocean floor.

Sharks' Kite-Shaped Relatives

Rays and skates may not look a lot like sharks. But these fish are actually close relatives. Both rays and skates have broad, flat bodies. They have tails and winglike pectoral fins. The shape of their bodies makes them look like swimming kites!

Rays, skates, and sharks all have skeletons made of cartilage. They also have paired fins and paired nostrils. They have dermal denticles and cylindrical or flattened bodies. Sharks, rays, and skates each have five to seven pairs of gill slits. They can all move both their upper and lower jaws.

Sharks are much older than their flatter relatives. Rays and skates first appeared about 150 million years ago. But scientists are beginning to wonder how much longer sharks will continue to rule Earth's seas.

There are about 500 different species of rays and skates.

CHAPTER 5

A Fragile Future

Sharks can live a long time in the wild. Some species have even been known to survive for up to 100 years! Many sharks' lives are being cut short, though.

A lot of people hunt sharks as a sport. Others kill them out of fear and a desire to keep beaches safe. Some people fish for sharks so they can sell their fins. Shark fins are a popular cooking ingredient in certain Asian countries. About 73 million sharks are killed for their fins every year.

Sometimes people harm sharks without meaning to. For instance, sharks often die when they become tangled in fishing nets. Also, overfishing and pollution are limiting their food supply.

Scientists believe that about 50 species of shark are currently in danger of extinction. It is important to remember that many sharks sit at the top of the ocean's food chain. This means that their extinction could have a huge effect on countless other forms of life.

It is very difficult for sharks to free themselves from fishing nets.

Saving Sharks

People are becoming more aware of the danger that sharks are in. Scientists are working hard to educate the public that sharks are not monsters. They are teaching divers, surfers, and swimmers that shark attacks are rare and can usually be avoided.

Other conservation efforts include creating tougher laws that limit how and why sharks can be hunted. Some people are even starting to use different kinds of fishing nets that are less likely to injure and kill sharks. Others are fighting to create human-free zones where no boats or swimmers are allowed. This gives sharks more room to search for food and reduces the risk that people will be attacked.

Sharks are an important and incredible part of our planet. Humans are their biggest threat. People alone have the power to make sure that sharks remain a fierce but fantastic part of Earth's future.

People still have a lot to learn about sharks and how to protect them.

Words to Know

adapt (uh-DAPT) — to change to fit a new setting or set of circumstances

aggressive (uh-GRESS-iv) — ready to fight or attack

camouflage (KAM-o-flaj) — coloring or body shape that allows an animal to blend in with its surroundings

cartilage (KAR-tih-lidj) — tough, elastic tissue

conservation (kon-sur-VAY-shun) — the act of protecting an environment and the living things in it

crustaceans (krus-TAY-shunz) — animals such as shrimp, crabs, lobsters, and crayfish that have jointed legs, hard shells, and no backbones

cylindrical (sil-IN-dri-kul) — having a tubelike shape

dermal denticles (DUR-muhl DEN-tih-kulz) — tough scales that make up shark skin

dorsal fins (DOR-suhl FINZ) — the fins located on the backs of many marine animals, such as dolphins and sharks

environments (en-VYE-ruhn-mints) — surroundings in which an animal lives or spends time

extinction (ik-STINGKT-shun) — being completely wiped off the planet

feeding frenzy (FEED-eng FREN-zee) — an aggressive group attack on prey by multiple animals

fossils (FOSS-uhlz) — the hardened remains of prehistoric plants and animals

friction (FRIK-shun) — the resistance of one object rubbing against another

gills (GILZ) — organs that remove oxygen from water to help fish and other underwater animals breathe

instincts (IN-stingktz) — natural behaviors or responses

lateral line (LAH-tuh-rul LINE) — a sense organ found on the side of the body that sharks use to detect vibrations and changes in water pressure

migrate (MY-grayt) — to move from one area to another

plankton (PLANGK-tun) — tiny underwater plants and animals that usually drift together in large numbers

pollution (puh-LOO-shuhn) — harmful materials that damage or contaminate the air, water, and soil

predators (PREH-duh-turz) — animals that live by hunting other animals for food

prehistoric (pree-his-TOR-ik) — from a time before history was recorded

prey (PRAY) — an animal that's hunted by another animal for food

serrated (SEHR-a-ted) — having a jagged edge

species (SPEE-sheez) — one of the groups into which animals and plants of the same genus are divided

streamlined (STREEM-lynd) — having a body form that offers little resistance to the flow of water

territorial (terr-uh-TOR-ee-uhl) — defensive of a certain area

vibrations (vy-BRAY-shunz) — rapid motions back and forth; how a shark can tell that another creature is near

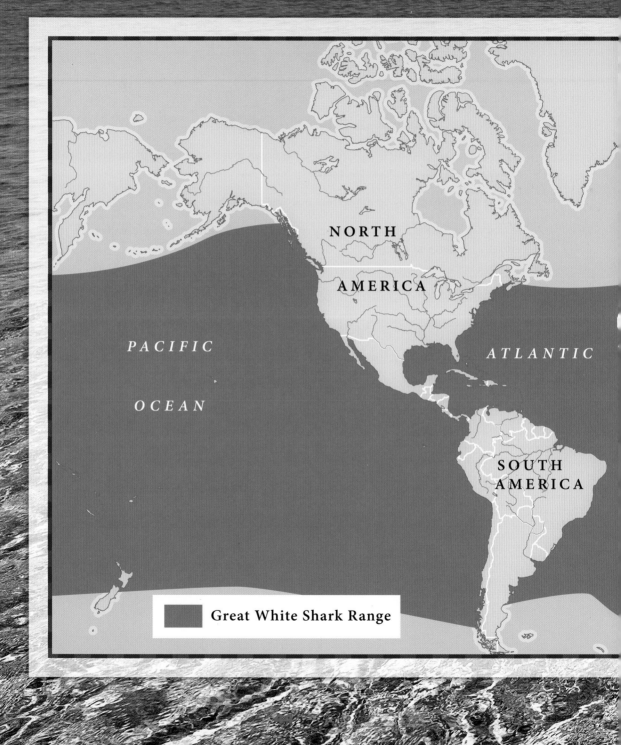

NORTH

AMERICA

PACIFIC

OCEAN

ATLANTIC

SOUTH
AMERICA

Great White Shark Range

Find Out More

Books

Bodden, Valerie. *Sharks*. Mankato, MN: Creative Education, 2010.

Clark, Willow. *Shark!* New York: Windmill Books, 2011.

Parker, Steve, and John Butler (illustrator). *Sharks*. New York: Windmill Books, 2011.

Web Sites

National Geographic Kids—Great White Sharks
www.kids.nationalgeographic.com/kids/animals/creaturefeature/great-white-shark
Check out photos, a video, and other interesting resources about great white sharks.

SeaWorld/Busch Gardens—Animals: Sharks
www.seaworld.org/animal-info/animal-bytes/animalia/eumetazoa/coelomates/
deuterostomes/chordata/craniata/chondrichthyes/selachii/sharks.htm
Read some fun facts and find out other information about sharks.

Visit this Scholastic web site for more information on sharks:
www.factsfornow.scholastic.com